High School Musicals™

DIRECTING

rosen publishing's
rosen central®

New York

Bethany Bezdecheck

For Ms. Jean Willoughby, my very first director

Published in 2010 by The Rosen Publishing Group, Inc.
29 East 21st Street, New York, NY 10010

First Edition

Library of Congress Cataloging-in-Publication Data

Bezdecheck, Bethany.
Directing / Bethany Bezdecheck.—1st ed.
        p. cm.—(High school musicals)
Includes bibliographical references and index.
ISBN-13: 978-1-4358-5259-4 (library binding)
ISBN-13: 978-1-4358-5532-8 (pbk)
ISBN-13: 978-1-4358-5533-5 (6 pack)
1. Musicals—Production and direction. I. Title.
MT955.B49 2009
792.602'33—dc22
                                        2008041598

Manufactured in Malaysia

Contents

INTRODUCTION

Mario has just spent an incredible evening at the theater. As the curtain comes down, he and those around him applaud and cheer wildly. After a minute, the curtain opens again, and the actors take the stage. They smile and bow as the crowd continues to roar. Mario shakes his head in amazement.

"What fabulous acting, singing, and dancing I just witnessed," he thinks to himself. Mario heads home, humming the catchy tunes he heard that night. He can still hear the drums in the orchestra pit. He can still see the dramatic shimmer of the spotlight. One thing's for certain: Mario now loves the theater! The only problem is, he's not sure he wants to be on stage.

Can you relate to this scenario? If so, directing could be the job for you. When watching a terrific group of actors on stage, it's

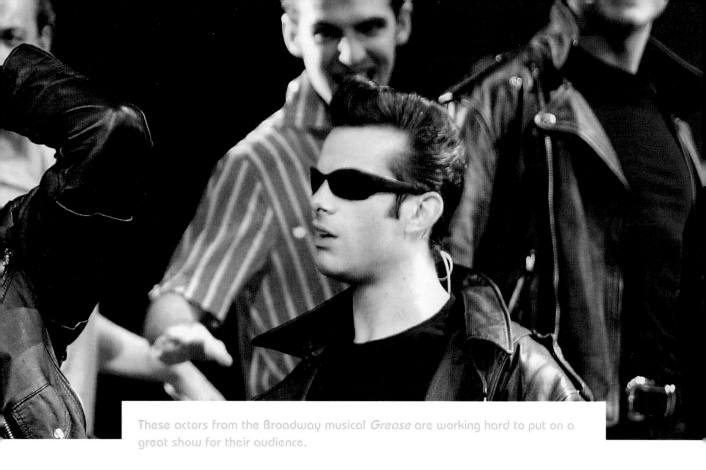

These actors from the Broadway musical *Grease* are working hard to put on a great show for their audience.

easy to forget that the most important role of all is one that takes place behind the scenes: the role of the director. Directing a high school musical is a great opportunity to find out if directing is the right career for you!

Setting the Stage

Before you take on your directorial duties, there are a few things you must know about theater in general. Having some background knowledge will make you a more confident and trustworthy director, and it will also make your upcoming job much easier.

It's hard to imagine a show coming together without a director. Who would schedule and run rehearsals? Who would tell the actors where to go and what to do? Who would make decisions about the overall look and feel of the show? As puzzling as these questions may be, until the twentieth century, most shows were rehearsed without directors. Instead, they were staged by the actors or the playwright. Things changed when theater became a more widespread, respectable form of art and entertainment. Shows were suddenly more elaborate and structured, and they required greater leadership and artistic influence. Directors were soon in demand.

As the director, you will be the person the actors turn to for guidance and support. Make sure you are well-informed and prepared at all times.

Today, there are many important components to a director's job, most likely more than you even realize. As the director of your high school musical, get ready to:

- Choose the show
- Analyze the script
- Convey your vision
- Run the auditions
- Select the cast

- Coach the actors
- Block the scenes

The duties listed above require a great deal of time and effort. However, few things are more satisfying than watching the curtain

The vocal director leads vocal exercises and warm-ups and gives tips on singing techniques like breath control and belting.

go up on a show you directed. And fortunately, a high school musical director rarely works alone. He or she receives lots of assistance. Let's take a look at some of the other people who play important roles in putting on a musical.

The Vocal Director

The vocal director teaches the musical numbers to the actors. He or she runs the singing portion of the audition and rehearsals, and helps the actors to develop their voices. The vocal director may serve as the pianist during rehearsals, and if there is an orchestra, he or she is often its conductor. You can recruit a music teacher or a fellow student who is both skilled in singing and playing the piano to serve as your vocal director.

The Choreographer

The choreographer plans and teaches the dance numbers to the actors. He or she also runs the dance portion of the audition and casts lead dancers for solo numbers. The person you pick to be your choreographer should be a talented dancer—with lots of creativity to share.

The Stage Manager

The stage manager assists the director during the audition and rehearsal process. He or she handles paperwork, takes notes, and works to make sure things are running smoothly and on time. The stage manager also oversees the technical crew. During the show, the stage manager tells the crew, via headset, when and what to do with the lights, sound, set, and curtain. This is referred to as "calling the show." It's necessary that the person you choose know a thing or two about technical theater. Someone who has previously served on a technical crew is a good choice for this leadership role.

The Set Designer

The set designer designs and creates the set, usually with the help of crew members. Your set designer should be creative and good with construction. Speak with art or shop teachers at your school when looking to recruit a set designer. They may have just the person in mind.

The Costume Designer

The costume designer designs the actors' costumes. He or she measures the actors and then creates or finds costumes based on these measurements. Do you know someone who is interested in fashion design or is good with a sewing machine? If so, speak to that person about working as your costume designer.

The Lighting Designer

The lighting designer chooses the look of the lighting and manages the lighting crew's efforts to achieve this look through light placement and structure. If your stage manager has previously served on the technical crew of a show at your school, he or she may know someone with the lighting skills necessary for this job.

The Technical Director and Crew

Members of the technical crew carry out the behind-the-scenes work, such as pulling the curtain, preparing the props, changing the set, and running the lights under the direction of the technical director. Your stage manager should recruit this important team. The technical director is usually a parent or teacher who can keep things running behind the scenes.

Although most of the people listed here play leadership roles behind the scenes, at the end of the day, they all report to the director. It is the director who dictates the style, theme, and atmosphere of the show. For example, the director may decide that the show should feel sad, yet dreamlike. If the costume designer then creates brightly colored, realistic costumes, he or she isn't doing the job well. Every aspect of the show must reflect the director's vision. Otherwise, the show will appear confusing and disjointed—and will make less of an impression on the audience.

When it comes to directing, not all work is done onstage with actors. An effective director takes time alone to come up with a strong overall vision for the show.

Creating a Vision

So, as the director, how do you make these important decisions about style, theme, and atmosphere? Such tasks may seem intimidating, but in actuality, they're not. In making these decisions, you are playing the role of an artist, and in art, there are no right or wrong answers. Of course,

it is necessary for you to know the proper definitions of the terms with which you will be working:

Style

"Style" refers to the genre, or artistic category, of the show. Some examples of theatrical styles are as follows:

- **Realism** In realism, the story is portrayed realistically. The set and costumes are lifelike, and the actors behave naturally.
- **Absurdism** In an absurdist show, nothing is truly as it seems. As in *Alice in Wonderland*, logic does not seem to exist. Things appear chaotic and larger than life.
- **Expressionism** There may be nothing absurd about the story of an expressionist piece of theater, but the set, lighting, and costumes are not entirely realistic.

An absurdist show may not appear realistic, but its artistic vision can cause an audience to feel very real emotions.

Instead, they are artistically altered to convey the story's theme.

Theme

The term "theme" is used to describe the most important idea of the story. Let's say you are directing a musical production of *Jack and the Beanstalk*. You might decide that the theme of your musical will be "The dangerous desire for riches." After all, Jack was willing to put his life on the line for a few golden eggs. Another theme for this show could be "The importance of family." This theme makes perfect sense if you decide that Jack stole in order to give his mother a better life. There is no right or wrong answer when it comes to choosing a theme. It all depends on your personal interpretation of the script.

Atmosphere

The overall feeling a show conveys is its atmosphere. As you read a script, think of adjectives you might use to describe the story. Is it haunting? Romantic? These adjectives represent perfect types of atmospheres.

Planning the Show

Once you have a good idea of what the style, theme, and atmosphere of your show will be, you must decide how to relay these things to the audience. Let's examine an example of how such decisions are made. Suppose you are putting on *Jack and the Beanstalk* and have chosen "The dangerous desire for riches" as the theme. Perhaps you want to take the show in a wild and creative direction, so absurdism is selected as a style. Next, begin to think about atmosphere. Maybe you feel that the theme of your show is dark and dangerous, so the atmosphere should be sinister.

You ask the set designer to create a beanstalk that looks as if it is made of sparkling coins and jewels. A beanstalk like this will hopefully support your theme of desiring riches. You then tell the lighting designer to light the stage in spooky colors, so that the atmosphere feels more sinister.

"Make the costumes as wild and crazy as you like," you tell the costume designer. "This is an absurdist musical, after all. Just make sure to keep the theme and atmosphere in mind."

The costume designer knows exactly what to do. He dresses the lady giant in an elaborate, gold-sequined ball gown, placing an oversized bejeweled crown on her head to demonstrate her wealth. Because the giant must look sinister, he tops her off with a long, scaly black cape fit for a wicked witch.

As you can see, there are lots of artistic decisions to be made! Of course, you first need to decide which musical to produce.

Selecting a Play

If you do not already know of any musicals, you will want to familiarize yourself with a few. You need to have a collection of ideas from which to pick. Go to your local library and ask if you can check out a few videotapes or DVDs of musicals. Make sure to tell the librarian that the musicals should be staged versions. Otherwise, you may end up with a handful of movie musicals. While most movie musicals were developed from Broadway shows, they are not performed on stage as pieces of theater. The Broadway musicals *Grease*, *Hairspray*, and *Dreamgirls* have all been made into popular movie musicals. These films may be enjoyable, but they

At the library, look up musicals using the computer search tool. Write down the call numbers for the books, DVDs, and CDs you want to check out.

do not always contain all the lines, songs, and characters from the original Broadway shows on which they were based.

You may also find scripts and soundtracks of musicals at the library. Although these materials will not show you how a certain musical can look on stage, they will provide you with the information necessary for familiarizing yourself with the show. Read a script to get an idea of the musical's story and characters. Then, listen to the soundtrack to see how you like the songs.

Of course, you will want to select a show that you like personally. But keep the following in mind when making your decision:

Appropriateness

Your school may not allow you to direct a show that someone finds inappropriate. Try to pick a show that is agreeable to an audience of all ages.

Number and gender of characters

Actors will appreciate your selecting a show with many characters. This means there will be more opportunities for each of them to have their moment in the spotlight. You may find that some shows have many parts for women but few for men, or vice versa. If you attend a school with both boys and girls, these types of shows are not for you. Not giving students of both genders the chance to shine on stage will leave people disappointed.

Popularity

Of course, your selection will generate more excitement if it is well known. The more popular the show, the greater your audition attendance and ticket sales will be. However, don't overlook lesser-known musicals. With a bit of ingenuity, any show could be a hit!

Scale

A large-scale musical, like *Wicked*, requires elaborate costumes, set pieces, and special effects. Putting on a show of this size requires a great deal of effort from everyone involved. Meanwhile, a small-scale musical, like *The Fantasticks*, requires very few technical elements. Select a show with the type of scale for which you have the time and effort.

Available talent

If there are a lot of skilled dancers at your school, you might want to showcase their talent by choosing a musical that features dancing, like *42nd Street* or *A Chorus Line*. Meanwhile, if very few students at your school have good singing voices, picking a show that requires skilled vocalists, like *The Phantom of the Opera*, is unwise. Keep the talent available at your high school in mind.

Royalties

If you are putting on a very popular Broadway musical, chances are you will have to pay royalties. Royalty payments go to the creators of the show. Each time their show is performed, the creators are entitled to payment, whether the performance is on a Broadway stage or in a high school auditorium. To find out if you must pay royalties, contact the rights provider of the show you wish to produce. Your school may be willing to provide you with some money with which to buy royalties. If not, you will want to consider only those musicals that do not require royalty payments. Neglecting to pay royalties is against the law.

If there are royalties attached to the show you select, you must fill out an application and make the necessary payments in order to receive copies of the script. Have an adult assist you with this process. You will need to order scripts for all the members of your cast because making photocopies without the permission of the publisher is illegal.

Once you have chosen your show, recruited your creative crew, ordered your scripts, and developed your vision, the stage is officially set for your big debut as a director. It's now time to meet the people with whom you will be spending the most amount of time these next few months: your actors!

Casting Call

Everyone knows that an audition is a nerve-wracking process for actors. What many people don't know is that it is a stressful situation for directors as well, especially if they are unprepared. Fortunately for you, this chapter will provide you with the tools necessary for running an accomplished, organized audition.

Preparing for Auditions

The first step in organizing an audition is to choose a time span and location. Auditions should occur right after school, when most students are available. Three hours is a good amount of time to devote to the process of auditioning. One hour can be concentrated on singing, one on dancing, and one on acting. It is up to the vocal director and the choreographer to organize and run the singing and dancing portions of the audition. As the director, you should be present at these times in order to help with casting

Actors may audition for you by reading a portion of a scene in small groups. Actors not onstage must sit quietly in the audience while awaiting their turn.

decisions. However, the portion of the audition you will be in absolute charge of is acting.

Your high school's theater or auditorium is the obvious choice for the location for auditions. Make sure to reserve the location for the appropriate date and time.

The actors that turn out for your audition can be referred to as the "talent pool." Have you ever heard the phrase "There are lots of fish in the sea"? You should want this phrase to apply to your audition. The bigger the talent pool, the more people you will have to choose from and the more likely it will be to find the perfect actors for your show. Therefore, aim to make your talent pool a talent sea by advertising the audition well. With your school's permission, hang some eye-catching posters in the halls. Ask if announcements can be made during the daily bulletin. Take out an ad in the school paper. And don't just target the drama club. You might be surprised by the amount of talent hiding out in the locker rooms, science lab, and band room.

When advertising auditions, make sure to include the following information: the title of the show, the time and location of the audition, how actors should dress and prepare for the audition, and who to contact for more information.

This level of preparation can be a big job for just one person. Make sure your stage manager, vocal director, and choreographer are willing to help you out. You may have a few friends that will volunteer to assist you as well. However, try not to involve those planning on auditioning themselves. They may expect you to favor them during the audition process.

Once recruiting is under way, you can prepare for the audition yourself. This operation is not always as exciting as you might think. For one thing, it involves creating, printing, and copying a great deal of documents. Again, make sure you recruit others to assist you.

The most important document you will create is the audition form. Each actor auditioning must fill one out. You will use this form to learn about, track, and take notes on the actors auditioning.

It is always a good idea to have plenty of extra copies on hand. You don't want to have to waste time by running out to make copies during the audition.

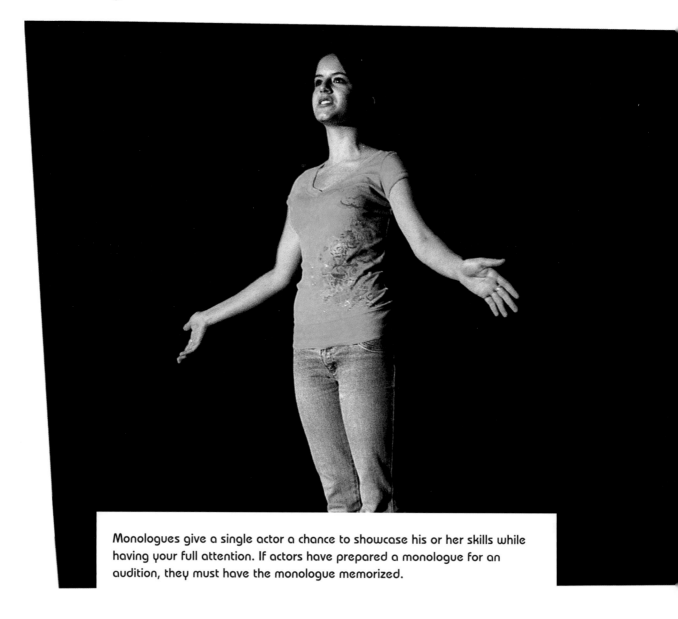

Monologues give a single actor a chance to showcase his or her skills while having your full attention. If actors have prepared a monologue for an audition, they must have the monologue memorized.

The second set of documents you will create depends on the way in which you would like the actors to perform for you. During an acting audition, actors perform either monologues or sides. A monologue is a speech given by a single character. A side is a selection of dialogue between two or more characters. Sides are almost always taken from the show for which the actors are auditioning. However, a director may request that actors come to the audition prepared to perform a monologue from a different show. As the actors recite their chosen monologues, the director will decide which of them have the acting skills necessary for playing a major role. He or she will then "call back" the most skilled actors and have them read for specific roles.

Judging monologues is a good

way to narrow down your talent pool. However, it is not always the best method for running an audition at a high school. The reason for this is that many of the actors auditioning will be fairly inexperienced. They may not understand what a monologue is or how to go about finding and rehearsing one. In these cases, having actors read sides is likely the better option.

Examine the script in order to select sides for your audition. At first, try to find scenes that include many different characters. The more people you can watch audition at once, the faster the process will go. Also, when choosing sides, make sure the dialogue is evenly distributed between the various characters. If one actor ends up doing most of the talking, you will be unable to judge the other actors effectively.

Once you have heard everybody read, you can have certain actors read again. At this point, you will want to select sides between just two or three major characters. You will know which actors you are interested in and will want to see these people read a good deal of lines belonging to a specific character. Here are some guidelines you can follow when selecting sides:

- Include all major characters. Each major character must be included in at least one side. If you leave a role out, you will leave the audition unsure of who is right for this part.
- Sides should be exciting! If your show is a drama, look for sides that contain conflict. Only the most talented actors will be able to make conflict compelling and believable. If the show is a comedy, look for sides that are especially funny. Using these sides will allow you to tell which actors are skilled comedians.
- There is such a thing as too many sides. Try not to have too many different sides. You will become confused,

Audition Form

Name:

When an actor is auditioning, you need to be able to easily locate his or her form. Therefore, the actor's name should be the first thing you see on this document.

General Information:

Contact info, should you need to get in touch with an actor.

Grade: Phone: E-mail:

Roles Desired:

Try to give actors the opportunity to audition for the roles that interest them.

1:

2:

3:

The vocal director will organize the singing audition, but it is useless to have an actor read for a part outside his or her vocal range. Take the time to learn which voice type each role requires.

Vocal Range:

Bass:____ Tenor:____ Alto:____ Soprano:____

Dance Experience:

If an actor has no dance experience, you may not want to spend time having him or her audition for a dancing role.

Ballet:____ Modern:____ Tap:____ Jazz:____

Please list any acting experience below, or attach a résumé:

Experienced actors are good candidates for major roles. Some of them may bring a résumé.

Director's Notes [Actors, please do not write within the box below]:

Use this space to take notes on the actors as they audition.

Here is an example of an audition form—a very important document. A proper audition form will let you keep track of the actors auditioning.

and the audition process will take much longer than it ought to.

Once you have selected your sides, make some copies of them. Count how many characters are involved in each side. This will be the number of copies you will have to make for that side. You may also want to make an extra copy for yourself. On each copy, highlight the lines belonging to one of the characters. The actor reading for this character will have an easier time following along if his or her lines stand out.

Your stage manager can hold on to the documents you have created. If he or she manages the paperwork during the audition, you will have more time to concentrate on the actors. The stage manager should pass out an audition form to the actors as they arrive. He or she should also keep track of the sides distributed, making sure each one is returned following a reading.

At the beginning of the acting audition, take a few minutes to welcome the actors. Thank them for their interest in the show and let them know they have ten to fifteen minutes to fill out their audition forms. Explain to them that they will be reading sides from the show and that everyone will have the opportunity to read at least once. Tell them that you will do your best to have them all read for at least one of the parts they are interested in but that this may not be possible.

As audition forms come in, work with the stage manager to match actors to sides. Base your decisions on the parts the actors are interested in, as well as their voice type and dance experience. An actor may want to read for a role that requires tap dancing, but if that person has no tap experience according to his or her form, it may not make sense for you to let the person read for this part. Do

This director is reviewing her notes from the audition with her team of leaders, which includes the choreographer and vocal director.

not worry about making every actor completely happy. Above all else, it is your responsibility to gather as much information as possible within the short time span of the audition.

Hand out several sides at once and have groups step off to the side or into a nearby hall to rehearse. Actors should be given enough time to read through the side twice—once to understand what is occurring in the scene, and a second time to work on developing their character. Have the stage manager round up the actors in the order in which they were handed sides. Each group will be brought to the stage to perform. While each group is performing, the stage manager should fetch the next group and instruct them to quietly await their turn offstage.

When a group of actors comes on stage, have them remind you of their names. While they are reading, you can jot down notes on their audition forms. At first, it may be easiest for you to scribble down other character names that you would like certain actors to read for. Another easy thing to do when you are watching many actors at once is to simply place the audition forms in two different piles. One pile will be for actors you are impressed with and would like to have read again. The other pile will be for actors you do not plan on considering for a major role.

So, what qualities should you look for while auditioning actors?

Projection

This is the actor's ability to be heard by the audience. Obviously, your audience will need to be able to hear the actors in order to understand the story. Therefore, good projection is an important skill for an actor to possess.

Diction

Actors need to be audible, but they also need to speak clearly. Watch out for actors who mumble or slur their words. This can be a difficult habit to try to break during the rehearsal process. "Enunciation" is a term that refers to the level of clarity with which an actor speaks.

These actors are using body language and facial expressions to convey the emotions of their characters. Based on this picture, how do you think their characters are feeling?

Stage presence

Stage presence is an actor's general manner on stage. An actor with good stage presence is noticeably confident and engaging. You will easily be able to picture this person glowing in the spotlight. An actor with poor stage presence, on the other hand, will either appear uncomfortable on stage or will fail to make an impression on you.

Believability

Any determined person can hop on stage and read lines loudly, clearly, and with confidence. Only skilled actors, however, can make their lines sound believable. Giving an actor a dramatic side is a good way to determine his or her level of believability.

Characterization

Actors must realize that they are playing characters, not themselves. This is called characterization. You should be able to see characters emerge during the audition, not the rehearsal process. If the character's "type" is not obvious from the side being read, let the actor reading the part know how he or she should behave when you first hand over the script.

Chemistry

When every actor has read once, you can have actors you are especially interested in read the sides containing just two or three characters. A pair of actors that seem to shine together on stage can be said to have good chemistry. Mix and match actors during the audition to find out which pairs have the best chemistry.

Manners

No matter how talented an actor is, you will not want to work with that person if he or she is disrespectful during the audition. Such actors will end up making the show less fun for everyone.

Callbacks

If you have decided which actors you are interested in for major roles, you may want to hold a callback. A callback is a separate audition attended by only those actors being considered for lead roles. If there are a lot of talented actors from which to choose, a callback will give you extra time to make an informed decision. However, if you know exactly who to cast in which part by the end of the audition, hosting a callback is unnecessary. Regardless, it is a good idea to reserve the theater for a second day ahead of time. If you do decide to have a callback, you will need the space to be available. You must also let the actors know early on that they may be required to return the next day so that they can make room for the callback in their schedules.

Before deciding which actors to call back, make sure to consult with the vocal director and choreographer. Is there anyone they would like to see sing and dance again? Listen to their thoughts on the actors you are especially interested in. What do they think of these actors' singing and dancing abilities? It is necessary for the three of you to work as a team to come up with the callback list.

If you are holding a callback, read the names of those actors you would like to see again at the end of the audition. Be sure to let the entire group know that actors not being called back may still be cast in the show. Explain that you simply do not need to see

Actors will be eager to check the cast list once it has been posted. Some will be thrilled, while others will be disappointed. Try not to let actors' emotions get the best of you at this time.

them again in order to make your decision. Finally, announce the location at which you will post the cast list once you have finally cast the show.

You can expect that actors will be excited and nervous the day the cast list is posted. You may be surprised to find that you are

excited and nervous as well! Most likely, you will be excited to start working with your cast and will be looking forward to congratulating them on their success. However, you may be nervous about hurting feelings. Some actors may approach you and ask why you did not choose them for a certain role. If this happens, be polite, yet honest. If people are angry, do not let them get you down. Remember that you did nothing wrong. Unfortunately, disappointing people is part of a director's job. Try to concentrate on the many positive things to come. You have a great show to look forward to!

Practice Makes Perfect

Once you have assembled your cast and crew, it's curtain up on the rehearsal process. High school musicals typically rehearse for two to three months. It's a good idea to create a rehearsal schedule as soon as possible to make sure your team has plenty of time to prepare.

Rehearsal schedules for each week must be shared with the cast during the week prior. This way, your actors will have enough time to arrange their schedules accordingly. Rather than waste paper and time by handing out copies of each week's schedule, post the document at a central location in your high school. Actors will be able to check the rehearsal schedule while on their way to class.

Make sure to work with the vocal director and choreographer when creating a rehearsal schedule. They will be in charge of the singing and dancing rehearsals. These rehearsals may be held on different days from the acting rehearsals, which you will lead. However, they may be held on the same date and time as your

Actors who are reading through a script should position themselves in a circle. This way, they will be better able to connect with each other.

acting rehearsals if the three of you do not plan on working with the same actors that day.

It is important to establish an encouraging, cooperative atmosphere among your cast early during the rehearsal process. Be sure that all actors attend the first rehearsal, which you will lead, so that they can meet their fellow cast members. It is a good idea to have the actors sit in a circle during this rehearsal so that everyone can be seen. Have the actors introduce themselves one by one. Each actor should give his or her name, as well as the name of the character he or she will be playing. Make sure to introduce yourself as well. For the next couple of months, you will be playing the most important part of all.

The first rehearsal is also the time for passing out copies of the script. Even those actors without speaking roles must be given a copy. Everyone, no matter how few lines they have, must familiarize themselves with the musical's sequence of events, or "run of show."

In all likelihood, your teachers don't let you write in your textbooks. However, you must encourage your actors to write in their scripts. Have them take notes in the margins as you give them directions. This way, they will be able to recall where to go, what to do, and how to behave as they follow along.

Once scripts have been passed out, have the cast participate in a "read-through." During a read-through, the script is read out loud, with each actor reading his or her part. This activity serves to introduce the group to the show. The actors will learn the plot, discover the characters, and hear the lyrics to the songs for the first time. Meanwhile, you will be given your first idea of how your actors will work together. Pay close attention during the read-through. Which actors will need to be coached on speaking up, or projecting? Do the actors sound natural when speaking with each other, or will certain pairs need help with their chemistry? Be sure to take notes on what you observe.

Rehearsal should be fun, but it should also be structured. From the very first rehearsal, you must establish certain ground rules to ensure that things run smoothly. Don't be so harsh that your actors won't want to work with you, but make certain they know you mean business.

Not every actor will need to attend every rehearsal. Sometimes, you will want to devote your time to a scene that includes only a

Rules for the Stage

You are the director, and it is crucial to the show that people listen to you. Here is a list of rules everyone must follow:

- Always be on time. No one wants to waste valuable rehearsal time waiting for actors to arrive.
- Remember to bring a pencil. If an actor doesn't have one, he or she won't be able to record your directions.
- Quiet offstage! It is disrespectful to talk while others are trying to rehearse. In addition, it's always good for actors to practice being quiet.
- Wear clothing you can move comfortably in. Baggy pants and tight skirts get in the way of stage movement, and high heels may cause an actor to trip and fall.
- If you have long hair, tie your hair back from your face. As the director, you will need to be able to see your actors' expressions.
- Treat everyone with respect. Drama should only be occurring during scenes. Offstage arguments and attitudes waste time and create a negative atmosphere.
- Stay in the rehearsal space.
- Follow directions. There is only one director: you. If an actor decides he or she is going to make up his or her own mind about what to do on stage, that person is not playing by the rules. Actors may make suggestions about their characters, but they should do so only after rehearsal.
- No food or drink. The last thing you want is for your principal to ban you from your rehearsal space because your actors have made a mess.
- Don't forget your script! It sounds obvious, but actors have been known to arrive at rehearsal without their scripts in hand. As the director, it's a good idea to bring an extra copy if you can spare one, but never encourage this bad habit.

few people. If certain actors are not needed, it may be a good time for them to work with the vocal director or choreographer. List the actors needed each day on the rehearsal schedule, and let them know whether or not they will be singing, dancing, or acting. Remind your cast to check the schedule often in case you have to make changes.

Have these actors come to rehearsal dressed appropriately? Untied shoelaces or baggy pants could cause an accident.

The first few weeks of acting rehearsals will be devoted to blocking. Blocking is the process of instructing your actors on when, where, and how to move. Try to block one to two scenes per rehearsal, calling only the actors included in these scenes.

Never arrive at a blocking rehearsal without knowing exactly how the scene at hand will be blocked. Your actors will not want to wait around for you while you think about what to have them to do. Take some time during the previous evening (after completing your homework, of course!) to plan.

Decoding Stage Directions

Before you begin to block, you must learn some simple stage directions. See the above diagram of a stage to help you with this task.

Don't worry— stage directions are

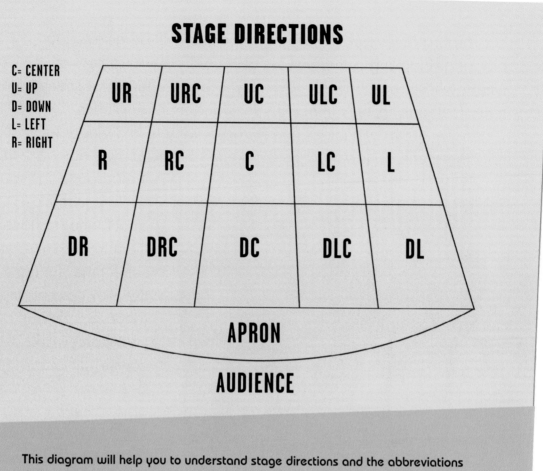

STAGE DIRECTIONS

C= CENTER
U= UP
D= DOWN
L= LEFT
R= RIGHT

UR	URC	UC	ULC	UL
R	RC	C	LC	L
DR	DRC	DC	DLC	DL

APRON

AUDIENCE

This diagram will help you to understand stage directions and the abbreviations that go along with them. You might want to make copies for the actors as well.

not as complicated as they look. Once you know what the letters above stand for, the diagram will make a lot more sense.

You will notice that all of the "U" for "up" letters are placed toward the back of the stage, far from the audience. This section of the stage is called upstage. Because it is more difficult for the audience to see and hear an actor who is upstage, it is not a good idea to have an actor stand here if he or she is especially important to a scene.

"D" is for "downstage." An actor that is downstage is close to the audience and will therefore have the majority of the audience's attention. Is there an actor you would like your audience to pay close attention to during the scene you are blocking? If so, you might want to place that actor downstage, at least for a portion of the time.

You may be thinking that "L" and "R" are for "leftstage" and "rightstage," but these terms are actually "stage left" and "stage right." These directions are based on the actor's point of view. If you are directing from the audience and you ask an actor to face stage left, he or she should turn toward his or her left, rather than yours.

Just like we read from left to right, we tend to watch a stage from left to right. Audience members will look stage right (their left) before they notice what is happening stage left. Therefore, actors are often instructed to enter from stage right, especially if the director wants an entrance to be noticed.

Finally, there is "C," or "center stage." This is where most of your action will occur. Even if you think a scene is important, its majority should not take place downstage. When actors are center stage, it is easier for the audience to take in the scene as a whole. The audience will be able to study the relationship between all the actors at once, as well as get a good look at the scenery and costumes, which help to convey the style, theme, and atmosphere.

Pencils especially come in handy during blocking rehearsals. Both you and your actors should note blocking in the margins of the scripts. Your actors probably will only need to write out blocking for their character. However, you must keep a written record of everyone's movements. This is the only way you will know to correct an actor if he or she is moving in the wrong direction. Although this may sound like a lot of writing, your knowledge of

A good director knows not to rely on his or her memory. It is important to have a written record of your blocking, as well as any notes you give to actors.

stage directions will make things easier on you. There is no need to write "downstage left" if you can simply write "DL." And if an actor is moving from one place to another, you can write "X" for cross. For example, if a character is crossing upstage right, you will note "X UR" at this point in the script, making sure to include that character's name.

Again, blocking should be planned prior to the rehearsal at which it is being taught. Of course, it is difficult to try out blocking ideas without any actors. When you are thinking about your blocking, you may want to use buttons, M&M's, or other small objects as actor substitutes. Move them around on a table to get an idea of how your blocking will look on stage.

Designing blocking depends on more than a character's current importance. You must also consider that character's motivation. Have you ever heard an actor say to a director, "What's my motivation?" This is a question directors hear a lot. Actors want to believe their character has a realistic reason, or motivation, to behave a certain way. This motivation must make sense to the audience as well, or they will not find the story believable. For example, a character cannot simply cross downstage because he needs to be heard. Such action must be paired with motivation. Perhaps the character is moving away from a situation with which he or she feels uncomfortable. Maybe he or she has spotted something in the distance and is moving downstage to get a better look. Whatever the motivation, it must make sense to both the actor and the audience.

Blocking also consists of "business." This term refers to what a character is doing with props or scenery. Slamming a door, pouring a cup of coffee, or washing a table are examples of business. During the first few rehearsals, actors can pantomime the business assigned to them, as props and scenery might not be available yet.

Blocking may not sound like a very artistic process, but you must keep your artistic vision in mind during this time. The style, theme, and atmosphere of your show should affect the decisions you make. For example, if you have chosen realism as your style, you will want your blocking to appear very realistic. If your show is absurdist, things can be a bit more silly.

There is no right or wrong way to block a scene. As the director, the choice of what to have the actors do is up to you. Blocking should be fun, and once it is done, your show will really start to come to life.

Curtain Up!

The second half of rehearsals will consist of run-throughs and dress rehearsals. During a run-through, actors will perform a series of scenes while working on their blocking and character development. A dress rehearsal is a run-through of the entire show, complete with costumes, props, scenery, lighting, and sound.

By the time run-throughs begin, actors should know all their songs and dance numbers. From here on out, there will be no more music or dance rehearsals, unless it is determined that certain numbers need extra work. As the director, you alone are in charge of the run-throughs and dress rehearsals. However, the vocal director and choreographer should be on hand to offer their expertise.

No longer do you need to spend your time dictating blocking to your actors. Now that you are in the run-through stage, you can sit back and really study your team's performance. Take notes during each run-through, paying close attention to the projection, diction,

At this stage in the rehearsal process, these actors have become comfortable as a team. They react to each other well and move with enthusiasm.

characterization, and chemistry of your cast. Also, remember to keep your style, theme, and atmosphere in mind. Your actors must be able to convey your artistic vision. Following each run-through, call all actors into the "house" (the portion of the theater in which the audience sits) and let them know your thoughts. Then, bring your notes with you to the next rehearsal. Re-read them and ask yourself whether or not the actors seem to be following your instructions.

If actors are having difficulty putting your notes into practice, feel free to take some extra time going over the issues at hand. Below are some solutions for common problems that you may find yourself needing to address.

Run-throughs should begin as strings of three to five scenes. Then, as things progress, the cast can run through whole acts and,

Take a look at this dress rehearsal. How well have the style, theme, and atmosphere of the show been conveyed using costumes and scenery?

finally, the entire show. Try and schedule your rehearsals so that your actors are running through both acts at least two weeks before the opening night. By this time, actors should also be "off book."

Once actors are off book, scripts are no longer allowed on stage. Make sure to tell your actors early on when the first off-book rehearsal will be. They will then work hard to memorize their lines by this

date. During the first couple of off-book rehearsals, actors may call for a line. If an actor forgets a line, he or she will call, "Line!" into the house. Your stage manager will then "feed" the actor the line by reading the beginning of it as a reminder. If you do not have a stage manager, have a friend or crew member feed lines to your actors. As the director, you should be watching the show, not reading the script.

Obviously, an actor who calls for a line every other

minute has not spent adequate time studying his or her part. Do not allow this sort of behavior. Not only is such an actor in danger of being unprepared for opening night, he or she is also wasting valuable rehearsal time by pausing to ask for lines. If need be, schedule an extra rehearsal to run lines with a forgetful actor alone. Hopefully, the actor will get the message and work harder at memorization.

Issues You Should Address as a Director

Poor projection. Sometimes, no matter how many notes on projection you give, one or two actors just can't seem to speak up. At this point, you should put the run-through on hold. Ask the actors to begin the scene again, this time with you sitting in the back of the house. Tell the actors that if you can't hear them from there, they must start over from the beginning. They will soon learn the volume at which they need to speak in order to be heard.

Poor diction. Even if an actor has no problem speaking up, you may still find it difficult to understand what he or she is saying. Print out a set of tongue twisters, and give it to those actors having trouble with their diction. Tongue twisters help to exercise the jaw, tongue, and lips, and are therefore a popular tool for actors looking to improve their speech.

Incorrect execution of blocking. If an actor moves to the wrong position on stage, he or she should go back and correct it. Changing one's position can occur without disrupting the entire show.

Weak characterization. The stronger a cast is as a whole, the more a weak actor stands out and disrupts the show. The most common cause of weak characterization is fear. Some actors are so afraid of looking silly that they put very little emotion into their performance. A good method for coaxing an actor out of his or her shell is providing him or her with positive reinforcement.

A typical musical should be about two hours long, including a half-hour intermission. Your actors should therefore take just forty-five minutes to run through each act. If it has been an hour since the beginning of a run-through and your actors are still rehearsing Act I, there is a problem with the pace of the show. Encourage your actors to get through their lines quickly, without neglecting their diction. Remind them that the longer they take to execute the run-through, the longer the rehearsal will last. One way to assist a slow cast is to have them run their lines together offstage. Have them sit around a table, and challenge them to recite their lines as quickly as possible, concentrating on picking up cues and not pausing between lines. They will find that it is easier to work on the pace of the show when they are not concentrating on their blocking as well. Once they are able to increase their speed offstage, have them return to running the show with blocking.

It is most common for a show to run at a slower pace at first. However, it is also possible for a show to run at too fast a pace. If your cast runs through an entire show in an hour, there may be a few things you need to think about. Were lines skipped? Did the actors take enough time to react? Would some additional action help tell the story? Make sure things are not moving so quickly that your audience will have difficulty understanding and enjoying the show.

As you can see, it is inevitable that things will go wrong during the rehearsal process. However, it is important for you to stay positive, no matter what occurs. As the director, it is up to you to cheer your actors on and fill them with positive energy. Inform them of their mistakes, but also celebrate their accomplishments. Remember, they are taking valuable time out of their lives to follow your directions.

Your actors must be as comfortable with the show as possible by the time of the first dress rehearsal. This is because the addition of costumes, props, and scenery can easily throw a show off course. Costumes may not fit, props may become misplaced, and scenery may fall apart. Plus, with all the additional distractions, it is likely that your actors will forget a few lines here and there. Should these types of mishaps occur, again, do not allow yourself to become frustrated. A dress rehearsal is

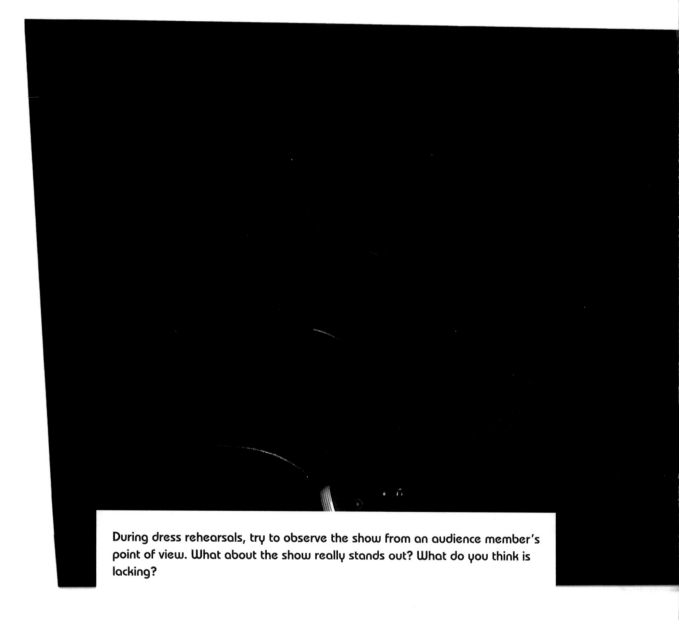

During dress rehearsals, try to observe the show from an audience member's point of view. What about the show really stands out? What do you think is lacking?

meant to be an opportunity to discover and fix such technical difficulties.

Since learning to work with the technical elements of a show can be time-consuming, it is best to schedule more than one dress rehearsal prior to opening night. When devising your schedule, keep in mind that dress rehearsals should run longer than other rehearsals: your actors will need extra time to put on their costumes and do their hair and makeup.

Observing a dress rehearsal is a good time for you to take notes on whether or not your artistic vision has been achieved. You will be able to tell if the lighting, scenery, and costumes accurately convey the style, theme, and atmosphere you have had in mind. If your desired results have not been achieved, feel free to share your feelings with the costume, set, and lighting designers. Together, you can brainstorm ways in which the technical aspects of the show can be improved.

Unless you absolutely must address a remaining issue, do not give notes following the final dress rehearsal. Your actors must be allowed to realize that they can no longer rely on your direction. In addition, the opening performance will have much better energy if the actors feel good about themselves, rather than critical. See the final rehearsal as a chance to sit back, relax, and admire your hard work. Put yourself in the audience's position and prepare to be entertained. You should walk away from the final rehearsal feeling happy and proud.

Directing a show is very hard work, but the payoff is definitely worth it. Now that you have mastered running an audition, blocking a show, and coaching a diverse group of actors, you can enjoy the smiles on the faces of the audience. Most likely, you will find that by the time the curtain closes on the final performance, you'll be ready to pick out your next script!

act A collection of scenes within a play or musical. Generally, productions will have two acts.

analyze To study by separating and considering parts of a whole.

apron The front section of the stage that extends beyond the curtain.

audition A process during which performers display their talents in an effort to be cast or hired.

convey To communicate an idea.

debut A first performance.

dialogue Language spoken by characters.

headset A combination of earphones and a microphone, a headset is worn on the head and is used to communicate with others not in the immediate area.

intermission An approximately fifteen-minute break during the two acts of a show. An intermission allows the technical crew to change the set and actors to change their costumes while members of the audience stretch their legs.

interpretation An individual belief, judgment, or communication.

lead A major role, or one that has many lines and is important to the story.

lyrics The words to a song.

pantomime To perform an action without using props.

playwright The writer of a script.

recruit To convince others to participate.

scene A section of a play or musical occurring at one time and location.

set Structures on stage designed to resemble an environment, such as a city or forest.

soundtrack A recorded collection of music belonging to a musical or movie.

vocalist Another word for singer.

wings The sides of the stage from which actors make their entrances.

American Alliance for Theatre and Education

7475 Wisconsin Avenue
Suite 300A
Bethesda, MD 20814
(301) 951-7977
Web site: http://www.aate.com
This is a professional organization that promotes drama and theater
education in the classroom.

Drama League

1520 8th Avenue
Suite 320
New York, NY 10018
(212) 244-9494
Web site: http://www.dramaleague.org
This service organization is for theater enthusiasts interested in enhancing
their understanding and experience of live theater, and it offers a
training program for emerging theater artists.

National Alliance for Musical Theatre

520 Eighth Avenue
Suite 301
New York, NY 10018
(212) 714-6668
Web site: http://www.namt.org
This organization promotes the creation, development, production,
presentation, and recognition of new and classic musicals.

Rodgers & Hammerstein Theatre Library
1065 Avenue of the Americas
Suite 2400
New York, NY 10018
(212) 541-6600
Web site: http://www.rnh.com
This organization publishes original theatrical, concert, and music
material and maintains copyrights on some of the classic material.

Society of Stage Directors and Choreographers
1501 Broadway
Suite 1701
New York, NY 10036
(212) 391-1070
Web site: http://www.ssdc.org
This is a national independent labor union that represents stage directors
and choreographers.

Web Sites

Due to the changing nature of Internet links, Rosen Publishing has
developed an online list of Web sites related to the subject of this
book. This site is updated regularly. Please use this link to access
the list:

http://www.rosenlinks.com/hsm/dir

Hal Leonard Corp. *Musical Theatre Anthology for Teens: Young Men's Edition*. New York, NY: Hal Leonard Corporation, 2004.

Hal Leonard Corp. *Musical Theatre Anthology for Teens: Young Women's Edition*. New York, NY: Hal Leonard Corporation, 2003.

Kislan, Richard. *The Musical: A Look at the American Musical Theater*. New York, NY: Applause Books, 2000.

Lee, Robert L. *Everything About Theatre! The Guidebook of Theatre Fundamentals*. Colorado Springs, CO: Meriwether Publishing, 1996.

Leiter, Simon L. *The Great Stage Directors: 100 Distinguished Careers of the Theater*. New York, NY: Facts on File, Inc., 1994.

Love, Douglas. *So You Want to Be a Star: A Complete Production Kit for Planning, Directing, and Performing Your Own Plays*. New York, NY: Harper Festival, 1993.

Rogers, Lynne. *Working in Show Business: Behind-the-Scenes Careers in Theater, Film, and Television*. New York: NY: Back Stage Books, 1998.

Shumacher, Thomas. *How Does a Show Go On? An Introduction to the Theater*. New York, NY: Disney Editions, 2007.

BIBLIOGRAPHY

Baldwin, Chris. *Stage Directing: A Practical Guide*. Marlborough, England: Crowood Press, 2004.

Bloom, Michael. *Thinking Like a Director: A Practical Handbook*. London, England: Faber & Faber, 2001.

Harvard University. "Rights and Royalties FAQ." Retrieved August 18, 2008 (http://www.fas.harvard.edu/~theatre/rights/rightsfaq.html).

Johnson, Margaret F. *The High School Drama Teacher's Survival Guide: A Complete Toolkit for Theatre Arts*. Colorado Springs, CO: Meriwether Publishing, 2007.

Kelly, Thomas. *The Back Stage Guide to Stage Management: Traditional and New Methods for Running a Show from First Rehearsal to Last Performance*. New York, NY: Back Stage Books, 1991.

Northern Arizona University. "Theatre of the Absurd." Retrieved August 1, 2008 (http://dana.ucc.nau.edu/~sek5/classpage.html).

Novak, Elaine Adams, and Deborah Novak. *Staging Musical Theatre: A Complete Guide for Directors, Choreographers, and Producers*. Cincinnati, OH: Betterway Books, 1996.

Novelly, Maria C. *Staging Musicals for Young Performers: How to Produce a Show in 36 Sessions or Less*. Colorado Springs, CO: Meriwether Publishing, 2004.

Page Crafter. "Stage Directions." Retrieved August 1, 2008 (http://pagecrafter.net/Drama/2stagedirections.html).

Pioneer Drama Service, Inc. "Frequently Asked Questions." Retrieved August 18, 2008 (http://www.pioneerdrama.com/faqs2.asp).

Walker, Julia A. "Expressionism and Modernism in the American Theatre." Retrieved September 4, 2008 (http://64.233.169.104/search?q=cache:fTpQ1vmvcOkJ:assets.cambridge.org/97805218/47476/frontmatter/9780521847476_frontmatter.pdf+theatre+Expressionism+Modernism&hl=en&ct=clnk&cd=18&gl=us).

Wise Geek. "What Does a Stage Manager Do?" Retrieved September 7, 2008 (http://www.wisegeek.com/what-does-a-stage-manager-do.htm).

INDEX

About the Author

As high school seniors, Bethany Bezdecheck and her twin sister had the opportunity to direct their own play, which went on to become an award-winning entry at California's Lanaea Theatre Festival. Today, Bezdecheck writes on a number of nonfiction topics and lives in New Jersey with her husband and her dog.

Photo Credits

Cover (background), pp.1, 44 Shutterstock.com; cover (inset) © www.istockphoto.com/Izabela Habur; pp. 4–5 Sandra Behne/Getty Images; p. 7 © Peter Hvizdak/The Image Works; pp. 8–9 © www.istockphoto.com/Lisa F. Young; pp. 12–13 © Jeffrey Fehder/Syracuse Newspapers/The Image Works; pp. 14, 31 © Michael McGarty; p. 17 © Anton Vengo/SuperStock; p. 22 © Dana White/Photo Edit; pp. 24–25 © Jim Commentucci/Syracuse Newspapers/The Image Works; p. 29 © Michael Newman/Photo Edit; pp. 34–35 © Spencer Grant/Photo Edit; p. 37 © Jim West/The Image Works; pp. 40–41 © Tiffany Warmowski/The Image Works; p. 47 © Chris Ware/The Image Works; pp. 48–49 © AP Images; pp. 52–52 Rubberball Productions/Getty Images.

Designer: Sam Zavieh; Editor: Bethany Bryan
Photo Researcher: Cindy Reiman